D1308309

EXPLORING OUR SOLAR SYSTEM

THE MOON

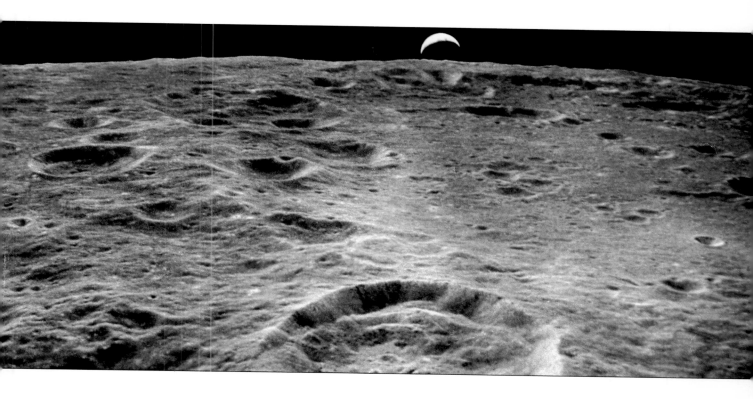

DAVID JEFFERIS

Crabtree

■ ABOUT THE MOON

The Moon is planet Earth's neighbor in space, our natural **satellite** that circles the Earth at a distance of nearly 239,000 miles (385,000 km).

The Moon is the only other world that humans have visited. So far, 12 astronauts have walked on the Moon, including Buzz Aldrin, shown on the left.

The Moon is far smaller than the Earth, but still has lots of territory to explore, with a land area about the same as Africa. And, although the Moon is smaller, its **gravity** pull affects the Earth by helping to cause the rise and fall of the ocean **tides**.

Crabtree Publishing Company
PMB 16A,
350 Fifth Avenue, Suite 3308
New York, NY 10118

616 Welland Avenue,
St. Catharines, Ontario
L2M 5V6

Editors: Ellen Rodger,
Adrianna Morganelli

Published by Crabtree Publishing
Company © 2008

Written and produced by:
David Jefferis/Buzz Books

Educational advisor:
Julie Stapleton

Science advisor:
Mat Irvine FBIS

■ ACKNOWLEDGEMENTS
We wish to thank all those people who have helped to create this publication. Information and images were supplied by:

Alpha Archive
Design Shop/Gavin Page
ESA European Space Agency
iStockphoto
JAXA Japanese Space Agency
JPL Jet Propulsion Laboratory
NASA Space Agency
UKSSDC UK Solar System Data Centre

Certain pictures courtesy of: HAO/SMM C/P project team and NASA. HAO is a division of the National Center for Atmospheric Research, which is supported by the National Science Foundation.

Lunar Appenines photo: Nordic Optical Telescope, Stockholm Observatory: M. Gålfalk, G. Olofsson, and H.G. Florén

Lunar interior diagram based on work by Calvin J. Hamilton

Bay of Fundy picture by Diane White Rosier

Library and Archives Canada Cataloguing in Publication

Jefferis, David   The moon : earth's neighbor / David Jefferis.

(Exploring our solar system) Includes index.
ISBN 978-0-7787-3731-5 (bound).
--ISBN 978-0-7787-3747-6 (pbk.)

1. Moon--Juvenile literature. I. Title. II. Series: Exploring our solar system (St. Catharines, Ont.)

QB582.J43 2008   j523.3   C2008-900978-9

Library of Congress Cataloging-in-Publication Data

Jefferis, David.
  The moon : earth's neighbor / David Jefferis.
    p. cm. -- (Exploring our solar system)
  Includes index.
    ISBN-13: 978-0-7787-3731-5 (rlb)
    ISBN-10: 0-7787-3731-4 (rlb)
    ISBN-13: 978-0-7787-3747-6 (pb)
    ISBN-10: 0-7787-3747-0 (pb)
  1. Moon--Juvenile literature. 2. Moon--Exploration--Juvenile literature.
  3. Moon--Orbit--Juvenile literature. 4. Moon--Phases--Juvenile literature.
  5. Moon--Observations--Juvenile literature. I. Title.
  QB582.J438 2008
  523.3--dc22
                                    2008004958

CONTENTS

■ WHAT IS THE MOON?

Our companion world is a rocky ball some 2,160 miles (3,476 km) across. The Moon has no air or liquid water, and no life of any sort.

■ HOW MUCH WOULD I WEIGH ON THE MOON?

Gravity is the force that attracts objects together. Its strength depends on how much matter, or **mass**, an object contains. The Moon is smaller than the Earth and has less matter, so its gravity is far weaker. On the Moon things weigh only one-sixth as much as they do on the bigger Earth.

The Moon is 2,160 miles (3,476 km) across

■ The Moon is about one quarter as wide as the Earth. It contains far less matter. It would take more than 80 Moons to match the Earth's mass.

■ WHY IS THERE NO AIR?

Because of the Moon's low gravity, any gases there have long ago drifted away from the surface, and off into space.

The Earth is 7,927 miles (12,756 km) across

— Moon

■ WHY DOES THE MOON SHINE?

The Moon has no light of its own, and shines only by reflected sunlight. Although a full Moon seems very bright, it is actually reflecting barely 7 percent of the Sun's rays toward the Earth.

The silvery colour of the Moon is an effect of contrast. Seen close-up, the surface looks more like a dirty gray beach.

■ The far side of the Moon was first photographed by the Russian Luna 3 probe, in 1959. Humans did not see it until the Apollo 8 flight of 1968.

■ This diagram shows the Earth and Moon to scale for size and distance. The Moon goes around the Earth in a near-circular path called an orbit, which takes 27.3 days to complete.
   The Moon's average distance from Earth is 238,900 miles (384,400 km), but it does vary a little. The furthest point is about 252,700 miles (406,700 km) away, the nearest point some 226,400 miles (364,400 km).

Earth-Moon distance 238,900 miles (384,400 km)

Earth

■ WHY DO WE SEE ONLY ONE FACE OF THE MOON?

This is because the Moon's rotation exactly matches the time that the Moon takes to circle the Earth – 27.3 days. So the same side of the Moon always faces us, and we never get to see the far side.

■ HOW DO WE KNOW ABOUT THE MOON'S FAR SIDE?

Early space probes flew around the back of the Moon in the 1960s. They sent back pictures of the far side. It looks similar to the face we can see, though there are fewer flat plains.

WOW!
The Moon also has an older, Latin name: "**Luna**", named after the Roman Moon goddess. We still use "lunar" to describe things about the Moon.

HOW OLD IS THE MOON?

Scientists who have examined Moon rocks reckon that our companion world is about 4.5 billion years old.

HOW DID THE MOON FORM?

It's still a bit of a puzzle, as no single idea gives a complete answer. The most popular theory is that a small planet, about one-third the size of the Earth, struck our world a glancing blow.

WOW!
The small planet that we think hit the Earth even has a name, Theia. It's thought that Theia and the Earth formed at about the same time.

The mighty impact "splashed off" rocks and other material into space. At first, they formed a huge ring around the Earth, but gradually collected together to form the Moon.

The planet's impact was massive. Some of the Earth's outer rocks hurtled off into space, to form a huge ring.

■ DID THE PLANET'S IMPACT KILL ANYTHING ON THE EARTH?

Absolutely not – the planet struck the Earth long before there was any life. However, if there had been any living things, they would have died instantly, as the heat of the explosion could have reached 18,000° F (10,000° C). That's hotter than the Sun's surface!

The earliest life on Earth is thought to have developed about one billion years after the Moon was formed – but no one really knows for sure yet.

■ HOW LONG DID THE EARTH HAVE A ROCKY RING?

Computer experiments have shown that rocks in such a ring could have come together to form the Moon less than 100 years after the impact. This early Moon was at first much closer to the Earth than today, and has been drifting away slowly ever since.

■ Moonrise would have been an amazing sight after it formed as a fiery new world. It has gradually moved away from the Earth, and today the Moon is moving away at a rate of about 1.5 inches (38 mm) every year.

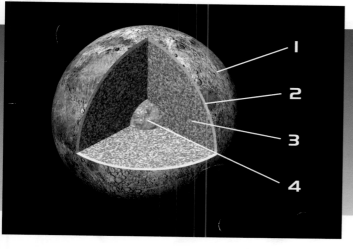

■ What we think the Moon looks like inside:

1 Surface.
2 Crust.
3 Mantle.
4 Core.

■ WHAT IS INSIDE TODAY'S MOON?

The Moon is made of several layers. Under the surface lies a rocky **crust**, some 12-62 miles (20-100 km) thick. Below this is the mostly solid **mantle**. The Moon's **core** is a hot mass, perhaps made mostly of molten iron.

■ HOW LONG IS A DAY ON THE MOON?

A complete lunar day lasts for 27.3 Earth-days, half in sunshine, half in darkness.

■ HOW HOT DOES IT GET AT NOON?

Temperatures climb quickly once the Sun comes up for nearly two weeks of daylight. The Moon has no air or clouds to give protection from the Sun's searing rays. In the open, rocks roast in average temperatures of about 220°F (105°C), hotter than a boiling kettle of water.

WOW!
Strange colored lights have sometimes been seen briefly on the surface. It's thought they may be made by gases leaking from deep inside the Moon.

■ This picture shows the baking daytime surface of the Moon. Running across the moonscape is a long sunken groove, or *graben*. Here a part of the surface has slipped below the land on either side.

■ IS THE MOON VERY COLD AT NIGHT?

Just as daylight hours are super hot, so temperatures plunge in the week-long chilly darkness. At night, rocks freeze at -310°F (-155°C). On Earth, the coldest place recorded is at the Vostok research base, in Antarctica. But even at an icy -129°F (-89°C), it's almost a spring day by comparison!

■ There may be water on the Moon, frozen as ice in shadowy areas near the lunar poles. If so, a future Moon base would be easier to run. Water could be mined locally instead of being flown all the way from Earth. This space probe is one of several built to try and find water-ice.

■ COULD I SEE OUR WORLD FROM THE MOON?

Yes. The Earth appears in the lunar sky like a beautiful blue marble. It looks big, too, about four times wider than the Moon appears from Earth. However, because the Moon always faces the Earth, our planet does not rise or set in the lunar sky. The Earth stays in the same place all the time.

■ The Earth hangs above the Moon in this picture, taken by a Japanese space probe.

WHAT ARE LUNAR PHASES?

The Moon's appearance in the sky changes from night to night. These different "shapes" are called its phases.

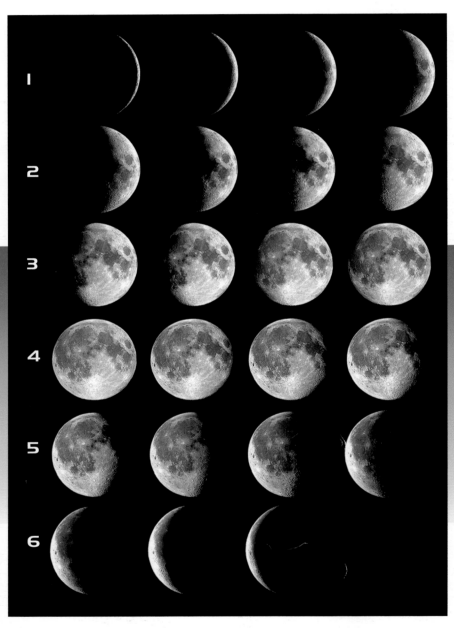

HOW DO PHASES CHANGE SHAPE?

It's not too difficult to grasp the idea of phases – they are simply the illuminated portions of the lunar sphere. As the Moon moves round in its orbit, so the Sun's rays gradually light up different parts of the surface.

These pictures show the complete range of phases as the Moon moves in its orbit around the Earth:
1 Waxing Crescent.
2 Crescent to First Quarter, also called a Half Moon.
3 Waxing Gibbous to Full Moon.
4 Full Moon to Waning Gibbous.
5 Gibbous to Third Quarter.
6 Waning Crescent to New Moon.
Note: A Crescent Moon is often incorrectly called a New Moon.

WHAT DOES A NEW MOON LOOK LIKE?

Actually, it is invisible! At this point in the Moon's orbit, the Sun is directly behind it. All we can view from Earth is the dark, unlit half.

WOW!
In folklore, the Moon's phases are linked with madness. So the word "lunatic" comes from this link, even though there is no evidence for it!

◾ WHAT CAUSES OCEAN TIDES?

Tides are the rising and falling of Earth's ocean surface, caused by the gravity pull of the Moon and the Sun on the oceans. If Earth had a single watery surface, then tides would be only knee-high. But in reality, water sloshes into narrow bays and inlets, and actual tides can reach higher than a house.

◾ Changing coastal geography means that high and low tides are different all over the world. The picture below shows a beached fishing boat at low tide in a Bay of Fundy harbor.

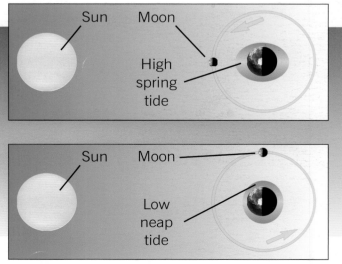

Sea at low tide

◾ WHERE ARE THE HIGHEST TIDES?

The Bay of Fundy, Canada, takes the tide record, with a range of around 53 ft (16 m) between high and low tides. But this is not Fundy's all-time highest tidal range. In 1868, winds from a huge storm boosted already high waters to give a towering tide height of more than 70 ft (21.6 m)!

◾ WHAT ARE SPRING AND NEAP TIDES?

When the Sun and Moon are lined up, their combined gravity pulls at the Earth, resulting in a high spring tide. When the Moon is further around in its orbit, the gravity pull of the Sun and the Moon tugs in different directions, giving a much lower, neap tide.

◾ Spring tides have nothing to do with the season. They are named for waters that "spring" up, higher than usual.

Sun   Moon

High spring tide

Sun   Moon

Low neap tide

■WHAT IS A BLOOD MOON?

This is a name for the Moon's coppery-red colour when it moves into the Earth's shadow during an eclipse.

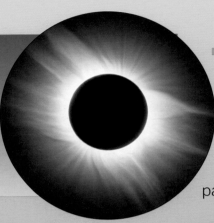

■ In an eclipse of the Sun, the Moon passes between the Sun and Earth. During a rare total eclipse (right), the Moon covers the Sun totally for a few minutes.

■ WHAT IS AN ECLIPSE?

There are two main kinds of eclipse. An eclipse of the Sun happens when the Moon passes between the Earth and the Sun, cutting off its light. The other is an eclipse of the Moon, when the Earth passes between the Sun and Moon.

■ HOW OFTEN DO LUNAR ECLIPSES HAPPEN?

Lunar eclipses take place whenever the Moon passes through the Earth's shadow. The Sun, Earth, and Moon have to line up exactly, which does not happen every time the Moon completes an orbit. Even so, an eclipse occurs at least twice a year, though it may just be a partial eclipse, when there is little or no change of colour.

WOW!
The Moon's color changes from eclipse to eclipse. If there is more dust in the Earth's air, the Moon appears a darker shade of red.

Moon changes color as it moves through the darkest part of the Earth's shadow

Earth's shadow starts to move across the Moon

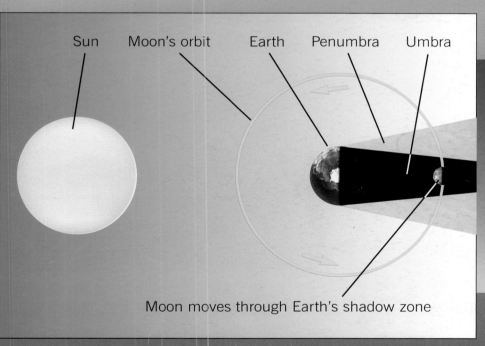

■ From start to finish, a lunar eclipse can last more than six hours. However, the Blood Moon part, through the darkest part of the Earth's shadow, is much briefer.
   The longest Blood Moon ever recorded lasted just over 107 minutes. It took place nearly 1,700 years ago.

■ HOW LONG DOES A LUNAR ECLIPSE LAST?

The Moon is moving constantly in its orbit around the Earth, and passes through the Earth's shadow at about 2,240 mph (3,600 km/h). At this speed, its journey through the darkest part of the Earth's shadow – called the **umbra** – normally lasts about an hour.

■ WHY DOES THE MOON TURN SHADES OF RED?

It's because much of the eclipsed moonlight is absorbed by Earth's dusty air. We see what's left of the light as reddish tones. It's the same effect that causes golden-red sunsets.

Sun   Moon's orbit   Earth   Penumbra   Umbra

Moon moves through Earth's shadow zone

■ The Earth's shadow is divided into two parts, the umbra and penumbra.
   In the deep shadow zone, called the umbra, there is no direct sunlight at all. In the outer shadow zone, the penumbra, the Sun's rays are blocked only partially.

■ WHO FIRST MAPPED THE MOON?

The first published drawing of the Moon was made by the Italian scientist Galileo Galilei, in 1610.

Galileo

■ This is Galileo's first sketch of 1610. His telescopes were simple instruments that did not enlarge much.

■ WHAT INSTRUMENTS DID GALILEO USE?

Galileo's telescopes were based on the designs of Dutchman Hans Lippershey. But they were not very powerful, giving about the same enlargement you get with a pair of modern binoculars. Even so, Galileo saw that the dark parts of the Moon were vast, flat areas. He also spotted various **craters** and mountain ranges. However, most of the Moon's features were named by a later Italian astronomer, Giovanni Riccioli, in 1651.

■ The U.S. Surveyor probes were part of careful preparations for the human landings made from 1969-1972.

■ WHEN DID SPACECRAFT FIRST FLY TO THE MOON?

The Russians led the way with Luna 1, a dustbin-sized craft that flew past the Moon in 1959. The next Russian probe, Luna 2, actually hit the Moon later the same year.

Throughout the 1960s, both Russia and the U.S. sent various space probes to the Moon. Some crashed, others landed safely.

Lunar Orbiter space probe

■ WHICH CRAFT MADE THE FIRST SAFE LANDING ON THE SURFACE?

After various probes had crash-landed, the Russian Luna 9 touched down gently, in 1966. It was also the first craft to send back pictures of the Moon to Earth.

WOW!
The second human landing on the Moon touched down close to the Surveyor 3 space probe (shown left), which had landed there two years earlier.

■ The two Lunokhod rovers trundled across the surface on eight wire wheels. Between them, the Lunokhods snapped more than 100,000 TV images, drove nearly 30 miles (48 km), and took many soil samples.

■ WHAT WAS THE FIRST MOON ROVER?

Throughout the 1960s, there was a "space race" between the U.S. and Russia, to be the first to land humans on the Moon. Russia lost the race, but carried on exploring with two Lunokhod ("moon walker") robots, sent to the Moon in 1970. Three other Russian Luna probes even managed to return to Earth, each bringing back a cupful of lunar soil for waiting scientists.

WHAT WAS THE EAGLE LANDER?

The *Eagle* was a two-man spacecraft, used to make the first crewed Moon landing on July 20, 1969.

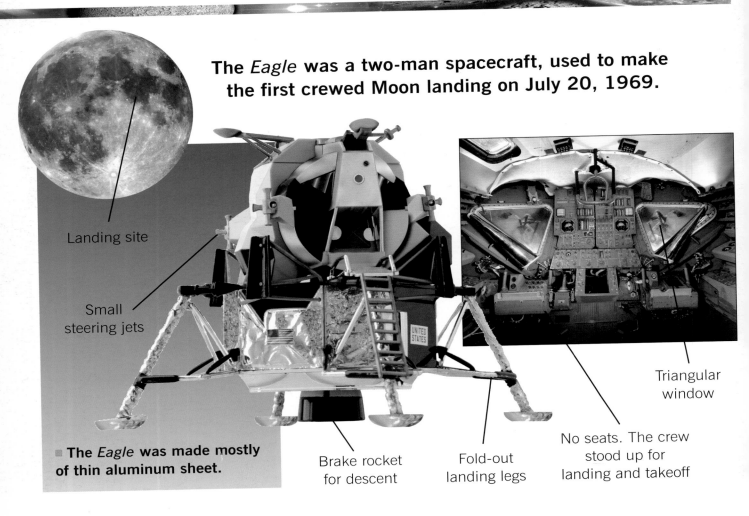

Landing site

Small steering jets

■ The *Eagle* was made mostly of thin aluminum sheet.

Brake rocket for descent

Fold-out landing legs

Triangular window

No seats. The crew stood up for landing and takeoff

■ WHO FLEW THE EAGLE LANDING MODULE?

The Landing Module (LM) had two crew, Neil Armstrong and Edwin "Buzz" Aldrin. A computer flew the craft toward the surface, but Armstrong had to take control, otherwise they would have missed the landing site and landed in an area strewn with large boulders.

WOW!
Human Moon flights were part of the U.S. **Apollo** program. The *Eagle* lander was launched into space by a huge, 360 ft (110 m) high Saturn V rocket.

■ WAS IT A DANGEROUS FLIGHT?

All spaceflights are dangerous, and the Moon missions are extremely so. If anything had gone seriously wrong, the astronauts would have been stranded with no hope of rescue.

■ HOW LONG WERE THEY ON THE MOON?

They stayed for 21 hours 36 minutes, and spent two-and-a-half hours exploring outside the spacecraft. Neil Armstrong took the first steps on the Moon, and said these words as he crunched on to the dusty surface, "That's one small step for a man, one giant leap for mankind."

■ WHAT ABOUT OTHER MOON FLIGHTS?

There were five more crewed Moon landings. The last lunar exploration, Apollo 17 of 1972, lasted just over three days.

■ Buzz Aldrin joined Armstrong on the surface, saying of this empty new world, "Beautiful. Beautiful. Magnificent desolation." Here Aldrin poses for Armstrong's camera, while standing next to the LM.

■ DOES THE MOON HAVE SEAS AND OCEANS?

The Moon has "seas" and "oceans," but they were misnamed by early astronomers, for there is no water. In fact, they are vast dry plains.

■ WHY DID EARLY ASTRONOMERS THINK THEY SAW WATER?

People studied the Moon for centuries before telescopes were invented. And to the unaided eye, the dark areas we can see do look a bit like water. They are still called after their Latin names "oceanus" (ocean), "mare" (sea), and "sinus" (bay).

■ HOW WERE THESE VAST DRY PLAINS FORMED?

Scientists think that the Moon's seas and oceans resulted from huge **meteor** strikes. Some of these were so big that they cracked the Moon's surface open. Scorching hot **lava** – molten rock – squirted out through the cracks to form flat-bottomed "seas" and "oceans."

■ **The Moon's seas and oceans are easily spotted – they are the dark areas. The arrow points to the landing site of Apollo 11 (see far right).**

■ **This is how we think the oceans were formed. Giant meteors cracked the surface like an eggshell (1). Hot molten rock from inside the Moon (2) poured up through the cracks and flooded the surface to form plains of lava when cool (3).**

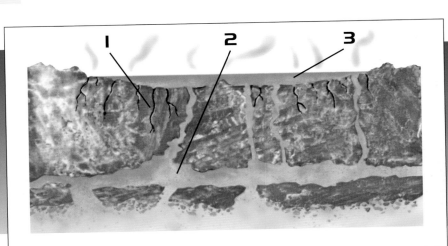

■ HOW OLD ARE THE OCEANS?

The last flows of molten lava flowed on the Moon a very long time ago – about 3 billion years! Since then, there has been little change. On the Moon there is no running water, wind, or weather to reshape the landscape.

In places, the lava plains are as much as 3 miles (5 km) deep.

WOW!
The Apollo 11 LM (pictured above) ran low on fuel as it approached the surface. There was less than 30 seconds fuel left in the tanks at touchdown!

■ Various instruments were left by astronauts, to take readings after their return to Earth. This instrument is a seismometer, designed to detect "moonquakes."

It found such 'quakes coming from about 200 miles (300 km) below the surface, and more of them from even deeper inside.

■ HOW BIG ARE THE MOON'S CRATERS?

The Moon is pitted with millions of craters. They range widely in size, from smaller than your hand, to huge features called basins.

■ HOW WERE CRATERS FORMED?

Most craters were made billions of years ago, soon after the Moon was formed. A hail of meteors pounded the surface, falling at up to 45 miles per second (72 km/sec). Most were tiny, but a few were miles across, and created huge craters.

■ DO METEORS STILL STRIKE THE MOON TODAY?

Yes, but nothing like the huge meteor storms that made the Moon's face we see today. At left is an artists's idea of how a small strike could look.

WOW!
Some craters are surrounded by a huge fan of "rays." These were made by light-colored material splashed out when the crater was formed.

■ The last human mission to the Moon was in December 1972. Here astronauts park their electric vehicle (in blue circle) next to Shorty crater in the Taurus mountain region. The crater was blasted out of the surface by a fist-sized meteor millions of years ago.

■ WHAT IS THE BIGGEST CRATER?

Bailly crater is the largest on the Moon's near side. Bailly is 188 miles (303 km) across, a distance that would take you more than three hours to travel in an automobile.

However, even Bailly is dwarfed by the **solar system**'s biggest known **impact zone**. This is the South Pole-Aitken Basin, on the Moon's far side. It stretches 1,300 miles (2,100 km) and is some 7.5 miles (12 km) deep.

■ This photo-mosaic of the Moon's North Pole was taken by the European SMART-1 spacecraft (shown at left). At the end of its mission, in 2006, SMART-1 crashed into the Moon on purpose. Scientists could then analyze the makeup of the dust cloud kicked up by the probe's impact.

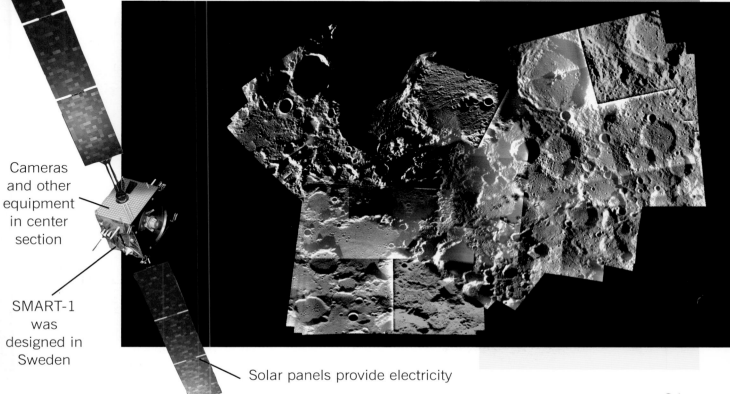

Cameras and other equipment in center section

SMART-1 was designed in Sweden

Solar panels provide electricity

HOW HIGH ARE LUNAR MOUNTAINS?

Hadley rille

The highest mountain we can see from Earth is Mons Huygens, a peak that rises nearly three miles (4.7 km) above the surrounding plains.

WHERE IS MONS HUYGENS?

It's a part of the Appenine mountain range, which was named after the mountains in Italy, here on Earth. It's not far from the landing site of the 1971 Apollo 15 mission.

WOW!

Before we explored the Moon closely, most scientists thought that lunar mountains would have sharp peaks. In reality, they are gently rounded.

The Appenine region includes the Hadley rille, a feature that looks much like a dry river bed.

■ WHAT ABOUT THE MOON'S FAR SIDE?

The far side has many more craters and rugged regions than the side we can see from the Earth. There are also fewer plains or seas.

Lowest parts of the South Pole-Aitken basin are colored blue

■ **Apollo 15 crew David Scott and James Irwin were the first to explore a hilly part of the Moon. They landed near Hadley rille and drove in an electric** lunar rover. **They stayed for three days and brought back to Earth 170 lb (77 kg) of Moon rocks.**

■ WHERE IS THE FAR SIDE'S HIGHEST POINT?

This is the South Pole-Aitken basin, with heights at the rim of about five miles (eight km). The lowest parts on the Moon are found in this area too, with land that dips nearly four miles (six km). These are the highest and lowest points anywhere on the Moon.

This area includes landslides and craters of all kinds

■ **The last Apollo flight was also to a rugged region in the Moon's Taurus mountains. The view below looks toward the Sculptured Hills.**

■ARE THERE OTHER MOONS?

Ganymede (Jupiter)

Titan (Saturn)

Callisto (Jupiter)

Io (Jupiter)

There are more than 240 moons circling other planets in the solar system. Mercury and Venus have none, but Saturn has more than 60!

■ ARE OTHER MOONS DIFFERENT FROM EARTH'S MOON?

The tiniest moons are little more than oversized chunks of rock. But some of the biggest moons, as shown above, are really mini-worlds – Callisto is bigger than the planet Mercury, and Io has volcanoes that spew gases far into space.

■ A space probe from Earth parachuted through the hazy air of Saturn's biggest moon, Titan, in 2005. Titan is the only moon to have a proper atmosphere, rather than just a few traces of gas. But you couldn't breathe the poisonous air, and Titan itself is an ultra-cold place that shivers at an icy -292°F (-180°C)

Earth

Moon (Earth)

Europa (Jupiter)

Triton (Neptune)

WHICH IS THE BIGGEST MOON?

This is Ganymede, which orbits the giant planet Jupiter. It was noted by Galileo, in 1610, and is called a Galilean moon for that reason. Like our own Moon, Ganymede has a **synchronous rotation**, meaning that one side always faces its parent planet.

■ This lineup shows the biggest moons in the solar system, to scale with the Earth and our own Moon. Jupiter's moon Io has more than 400 volcanoes and 100-plus mountains. Some of these are taller than Mt Everest, the highest peak on Earth.

AND THE SMALLEST MOON?

There is no real answer to this, as the smallest moons are just a few hundred feet across, making their exact size difficult to measure. However, the ringed planet Saturn has more than 60 moons, some of which are tiny. And there are probably dozens more smaller "moonlets" waiting to be discovered.

WHERE ARE THE MOONS FEAR AND PANIC?

These are the English names for the two small moons of Mars. They were named after the Greek gods Phobos (fear) and Deimos (panic).

WOW!
The solar system has eight major planets, which orbit the Sun at various distances. In turn, moons orbit around their parent planets.

■ HOW CAN I OBSERVE THE MOON?

The Moon is far and away the best space object to view at night. A small telescope gives a grandstand view, but even a cheap pair of binoculars will give fascinating viewing.

■ CAN I PHOTOGRAPH THE MOON EASILY?

It's not difficult if you have the right camera. First, you need a zoom lens to get a good closeup image. Second, you need manual exposure controls, or the Moon will probably show up only as a boring white blur. Third, use a tripod. This gives your camera a solid support to avoid blurred or fuzzy pictures.

WOW!
The best size of binoculars to use is either 8x30 or 10x50. The first number is the enlargement you get, the second the size of the lens.

■ WHAT IS MULTIPLE EXPOSURE?

It's a way of taking pictures like the one above, in which you can combine several images into a single picture, as the Moon moves across the night sky. The six shots shown were taken at two-minute intervals.

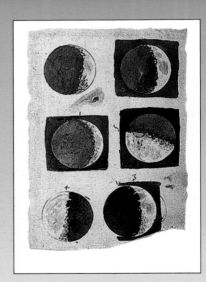

■ Galileo sketched the Moon some 400 years ago. You can make similar drawings, or take photos if you have suitable equipment.

A six-inch telescope is among the very best ways to go Moon gazing. It gives such a huge enlargement that the view is almost like flying over the cratered surface. A telescope is a pricey piece of kit though, so cheaper binoculars make a good alternative.

A sturdy tripod keeps the telescope steady.

Mare Imbrium (Sea of Rains)

Mare Serenitatis (Sea of Serenity)

Mare Crisium (Sea of Crises)

Copernicus (crater)

Oceanus Procellarum (Ocean of Storms)

■ WHAT CAN I SEE ON THE MOON?

There's a lot on view, and all you need is a clear night. The seas and oceans are easy enough to spot, as are craters and mountain ranges. These are best seen at Half Moon, when sidelighting from the Sun helps to show them up in sharp detail.

Appenines (mountains)

Mare Tranquilitatis (Sea of Tranquility)

Mare Nectaris (Sea of Nectar)

Mare Nubium (Sea of Clouds)

Bailly (crater)

Tycho (**ray crater**)

Mare Foecunditatis (Sea of Fecundity)

■ FACTS AND FIGURES

■ MOON STATISTICS

Diameter

2,160 miles (3,476 km), making the Moon about one-quarter as wide as the Earth.

Time to rotate

27.3 days average. The Moon always turns the same face to the Earth, so its day is as long as its orbit. Sunlight and darkness are the same, nearly a fortnight each.

Distance from Earth

238,900 miles (384,400 km) average. The Moon's reflected sunlight takes about 1.3 seconds to travel across space to the Earth, as do radio signals to and from spacecraft that are on or near the Moon.

Composition

Moon soil is made up of 42 percent oxygen, 21 percent silicon, and 13 percent iron. Other minerals include calcium, aluminum, and magnesium.

Temperature

The Moon's surface temperature in daytime is about 220°F (105°C). At night or in shadow, temperatures sink to about -310°F (-155°C).

Mass

The Moon is about 1/81 the mass of the larger Earth.

Surface gravity

Here on Earth we live under a force of one gravity, or 1G. If you could stand on the Moon, it would pull down on you with a force of just one-sixth 1G.

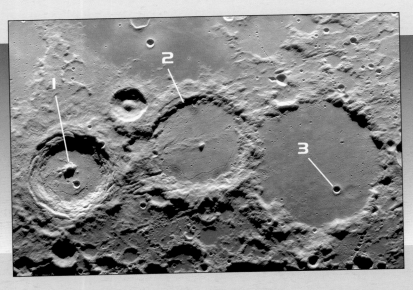

□ **Many lunar craters have features like these:**
1 A central peak, caused by the mighty impact.
2 A circular rim wall forms the outside of the crater.
3 Inside the crater, there may be other, smaller craters, made by later meteor impacts.

1

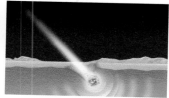
2

3

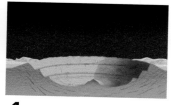
4

■ The Moon has about 500,000 craters bigger than 1000 yards (1 km) across. They were formed by meteor impacts.

The diagrams above show how we think such lunar craters are formed:

1 Meteor falls at very high speed.
2 It punches through the surface, and sends out shock waves through the soil.
3 The explosion blows out a massive hole.
4 A circular rim wall with central peak are formed, to make the new crater.

HOW LONG DOES IT TAKE TO REACH THE MOON?

To get a good idea of the distance, think of traveling in an automobile at 60 mph (100 km/h). This way it would take you about six months nonstop to arrive on the Moon.

Apollo crews took about three days to cross space between Earth and Moon.

WHAT WAS THE APOLLO PROGRAM?

This was the 1960s U.S. human space program, started with one aim – to land a person on the Moon before anyone else. Apollo was a great success – the first landing was made in 1969, and was followed by five more landings, the last one being Apollo 17, in December 1972. However, the Apollo 13 crew did not make a landing. In fact, they were lucky to return alive, after an oxygen tank exploded on the way to the Moon.

WILL THERE BE MORE MOON FLIGHTS IN THE FUTURE?

Several countries, including the U.S., are now planning to return to the Moon. The first new landings should be after the year 2015.

■ The first men on the Moon were Neil Armstrong (left) and Buzz Aldrin (right). Michael Collins stayed in orbit above the Moon in a Command Module spacecraft. The crew returned to Earth in this, leaving the *Eagle* behind.

■ GLOSSARY

Here are explanations for many of the terms used in this book.

Apollo The U.S. project to send humans to the Moon was called the Apollo space program. The program was named after the Greek sun god.

■ **The crater Tycho is 53 miles (85 km) across. Around it are long rays in a star-like pattern. As big craters go, Tycho is a youngster, at "only" 108 million years old.**

Command Module The control section of a spacecraft. In the Apollo moonship, the Command Module stayed in orbit, while the Landing Module flew down to the Moon.

Core The center of the Moon, thought to be made of hot, molten iron.

Crater A bowl-shaped hollow on the surface of the Moon. Typically caused by the impact of a high-speed meteor.

Crust The outermost layer of rock of the Moon, or a planet such as the Earth. At its thinnest, the Moon's crust is just 12 miles (20 km) deep.

Eclipse When one space object obscures the light from another. In an eclipse of the Moon, the Earth passes between the Sun and Moon. In an eclipse of the Sun, the Moon passes between Sun and Earth. Such eclipses may be partial or total.

Graben A section of the Moon's crust that has sunk between the ground on either side. Also known as a rift.

Gravity The universal force of attraction between all objects.

Impact zone General area where meteors have hit the surface.

Lava Molten rock that is so hot it can flow as a fiery liquid.

Luna Roman word for the Moon.

Lunar rover A vehicle for driving on the Moon. Russia sent two robotic Lunokhods. Apollo astronauts on several missions used a two-seat rover to go beyond walking distance.

Mantle The part of the Moon's interior between the outer crust and the central core.

■ **A huge Saturn V rocket launched Apollo missions to the Moon.**
1 Three-man Command Module.
2 Landing Module stored here.

Mass The quantity of matter that an object contains.

Meteor A chunk of space rock, often made of nickel or iron. If one hits a planet, or the Moon, it is then called a meteorite.

Oceanus The Roman name for an ocean, still used for various places on the Moon, as are Mare (sea) and Sinus (bay).

Orbit The curving path a space object takes around a more massive one. The Moon orbits the bigger Earth, as the Earth orbits the huge Sun.

Phase Apparent lunar change of shape when lit from different angles.

Ray crater A crater that is surrounded by a star-like pattern of light-colored rays. Thought to be material thrown up by a huge meteor strike.

Rille A narrow channel on the Moon's surface, similar to a graben.

Satellite Any space object that orbits a bigger one. It can be a natural satellite, such as the Moon, or an artificial one, such as a space station.

Solar system Name for the Sun and the various space objects that circle it. These include the eight major planets, dwarf planets, moons, plus billions of rocks, and space dust.

Synchronous rotation When a moon keeps one side facing its parent planet as it circles in orbit.

Tide The rising and falling of the oceans, due to the gravity pull of the Moon and the Sun. When the Sun and Moon are in line, their gravity combines to give very high spring tides. When they are apart, tides are lower and called neap tides.

Umbra The dark central part of a shadow area. The penumbra is lighter and surrounds the umbra.

☐ Apollo 15 astronauts drove in an electric lunar rover when they explored the area around Hadley rille.

■ GOING FURTHER

Using the Internet is a great way to expand your knowledge of the Moon.

Your first visit should be to the site of the U.S. space agency, NASA. Its site shows almost everything to do with space, from the history of spaceflight to astronomy and plans for future missions to the Moon.

There are also websites that give detailed space news. Try these sites to start with:

http://www.nasa.gov	A huge site.
http://www.spacedaily.com	Good for news.
http://www.space.com/moon	Lots of info.
http://www.google.com/moon	Zoom in up close!
http://stardate.org/nightsky/moon	Phase planner.

■INDEX

Printed in the U.S.A.